Tree Houses

Tree Houses

ESCAPE TO THE CANOPY

images
Publishing

Contents

7 Introduction

Escape to the canopy

12 **Suspended disbelief** | Sweden

20 **Embedded in nature** | United States

26 **Arctic experience** | Finland

34 **Common dream** | Switzerland

42 **Lofty escape** | Sweden

50 **Tuscan delight** | Italy

56 **Chapel on the river** | United States

60 **Treetop castles** | France

68 **Inspired geometry** | South Africa

76 **Jungle living** | Costa Rica

82 **Designer hideout** | Australia

88 **Across the canopy** | Canada

94 **Woodland wonder** | United States

102 **Connected to nature** | Mexico

108 **Patchwork of glass** | United States

114 **Lakeside living** | United States

120 **Lavender fields** | Italy

126 **Simple pleasures** | Russia

130 **Uplifting experiment** | Indonesia

138 **Cozy tranquility** | Denmark

144 **Reflective ambitions** | Sweden

152 **Pinecone peek-a-boo** | Italy

160 **Summer garden retreat** | United Kingdom

166 **Building on traditions** | Mexico

174 **Thermal motivation** | Portugal

180 **Playing with the aspect** | France

188 **Pine design** | Portugal

194 **Backyard beauty** | Portugal

200 **Counting on the view** | Germany

208 **Out of this world** | China

216 **Over the water** | Germany

222 **Urban double act** | Germany

228 **Magic in the woods** | United Kingdom

238 **Diner's delight** | New Zealand

246 **Rain and shine** | United States

254 Project credits

Introduction

I distinctly remember my childhood, growing up on a New Zealand farm with eight siblings creating imaginary spaces and tree houses together, to escape to the canopy. Inspired by fairy-tales (yes, also for boys), comics, and early black-and-white television shows such as *Flash Gordon* and *Lost in Space*, we used whatever we could find. From broken branches to leftover (and not so leftover!) building materials and packing cases, using hammer-straightened rusted nails and bailing twine to secure and connect our creations. What we lacked in experience and knowledge, we complemented with huge doses of enthusiasm.

Like many tree-house designers, my inspiration comes from tapping into my inner child's world and those early experiences. It is a place where innocence, inquisitiveness, nonjudgment, and the thrill of accomplishing something adventurous and sometimes outrageous, thrives. And now, the once basic tree house is a collision of many elements and responses, embodied across creativity and art, commercial realities and building technologies.

We had no understanding of material technology and engineering as kids. Spans were made from planks of (usually) unsuitable wood to create floors, walls, and roofs. When the tree house collapsed from its perch high-up in the branches, we learnt quickly which materials were too weak to take one child, let alone three or more. Aesthetics didn't rate highly. We were more interested in constructing a tree house that stayed together for more than a day and with practice and time, they did. Waterproofing was never a consideration, just an annoyance when passing showers forced us inside or saturated our uncovered sandwiches and homemade ANZAC cookies. However, this was eclipsed by the exhilarating feeling of being up high, hidden from view with vast outlooks over the local paddocks and cows, and building without any plans.

There are still no rules for building in trees; however, there is a boundary of care and safety that is crossed immediately when used in the real world. Our childhood memories and scars are evidence of the consequences of not getting it right. Materials, structural options, methodologies, and budgets enable a greater choice for design. And finally, the construction—using big-boy's toys for the build—something I did not have access to as a kid, much to my parent's relief. A tower crane would have reached the tallest branches, but that is a long way to fall when the floorboards collapse!

As evidenced by the stunning tree houses showcased here, the essence of tree-house design in the real world remains emotive, limitless, and has universal appeal. Shape, form, materials, and textures inspire and capture the heart, whether it be beautiful timbers, raw and exquisitely finished, or eco-charcoal external finishes, such as those used in the Treehouse (Playing with the aspect) in France, or the contrasting look of the modern steel and glass seen in Treehouse Solling (Over the water) in Germany. ACES Treehouse (Embedded in nature), a simply sophisticated learning platform in Aspen, displays a beautiful wooden framework, while the Danish hotel suite, LOVTAG (Cozy tranquility), is inspired by the local environment. Other examples, such as Yoki Treehouse (Rain and shine) in Texas provide a clear demonstration of working with the tree configuration, while Urban Treehouse (Urban double act) in Berlin displays a pre-determined aesthetic in its design. Whether the final design is traditional or contemporary, working with nature, or something quite random—it is always inspired.

Other designs included in this collection are simply sculptural delights, such as Tree Snake House (Thermal motivation) in Portugal or where the structure has been integrated into its backdrop, as we see in Tree Houses@ACRE (Building on traditions) in Mexico.

The designs here beautifully integrate with equally stunning environments, a duty of the designer to create naturally belonging structures, whether an 'Arctic Experience' or something to suit the tropical conditions of 'Jungle Living' in Costa Rica.

From the simplest to more complex and sophisticated designs, tree houses are built to captivate the minds of young and old, rekindling fond childhood memories and inspiring memories yet to be created. It is our responsibility to encourage new generations to use their imaginations wherever possible. Creativity lies in the foraging of materials, fixings, and tools, learning from trial and error, and embracing nature and the elements that impact our lives. That is what learning is about. And my childhood experience in constructing tree houses with my siblings inspired me to become an architect.

Peter Eising is the managing director at the award-winning firm Architects Pacific Environments, based in Auckland, New Zealand. Peter's experience reflects a strong focus on residential/lifestyle work, covering a wide range of project types that also include resorts and lodges, master planning, urban design, retail, low-cost and affordable housing, and civic developments.

Escape to the canopy

Suspended disbelief

Another addition to the renowned Treehotel in northern Sweden, The 7th Room rises majestically on twelve columns and into the tree canopy, offering views of the Lapland landscape. With its focus on the surrounding nature, the design features large windows, a netted terrace suspended above the forest floor, and a tree stretching up through the cabin. The boundaries between indoors and outdoors are blurred, making the arboreal hotel room part of the forest.

Designed to be a celebration of the traditional Nordic cabin, the wooden façade is clad with pine boards. The surface is burnt to create a dark and maintenance-free façade. The indoor flooring is made from ash wood, while birch plywood is used for the interior walls. With two bedrooms, a social lounge area, bathroom, and the airy terrace, the cabin accommodates up to five guests. The lounge area is located on the lower floor, while the bedrooms are on the upper level with the beds embedded in the floor. A staircase brings guests from the ground and up into the cabin, along with a small lift for transporting luggage.

With the primary aim of bringing people and nature closer together, the structure playfully blends the distinction between indoors and outdoors, by way of the double-layered net. The daring can sleep outside on the net under the starry sky. But guests who remain indoors can also enjoy the celestial splendor, with expansive, openable skylights in both bedrooms. Scandinavian-designed furniture and lighting create a soothing and minimalist atmosphere. A north-facing floor-to-ceiling window gives you the best chance to see the Aurora Borealis on a clear day, giving this social space the name the Northern Light lounge.

THE 7TH ROOM (SNØHETTA), Harads, Sweden

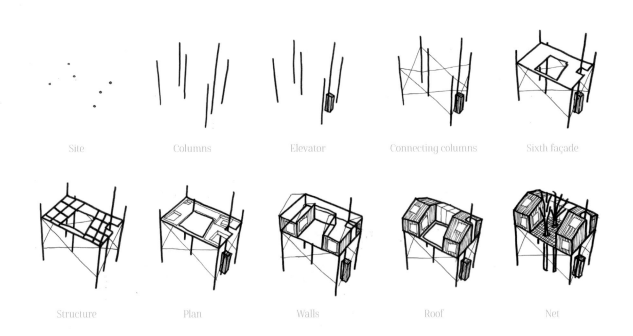

Site

Columns

Elevator

Connecting columns

Sixth façade

Structure

Plan

Walls

Roof

Net

Embedded in nature

Hallam Lake, a 25-acre (10-hectare) nature preserve and environmental learning center, is home to the Aspen Center for Environmental Studies (ACES), and is open to the public year-round, providing an inspiring setting for ACES' many educational and naturalist programs. And it now contains a newly designed tree house-like structure to enable visitors to get up close to nature.

After years of weathering and decay, the original platform on the site was redesigned by Charles Cunniffe Architects in collaboration with ACES. The new design and construction used the original four-column structure. The goal was to create different stations to enjoy the various aspects of the ecology. The sensitive design makes it seem as if the structure belongs in its environs, and is beckoning you in. The finished product is the result of the firm and construction staff donating time and materials to produce a truly community-based project.

Marine-grade plywood meticulously formed with a CNC router forms the exterior, with polygal used for a stunning visual relief. Ascending the steps to the upper level of the platform allows viewers to watch the swallows in search of insects, the American dippers diving underwater, deer, foxes, bears, Golden eagles, Great horned owls, and Red-tailed hawks; all the while designed so children and adults alike can view without scaring the wildlife. Vertical elements in the cottonwood bark were the color and orientation inspiration, and the use of the existing materials harks back to ACES and CCA's philosophy of reuse. ACES naturalists conduct ecology classes at this "outdoor classroom," and by placing students in the heart of the ecological space, they can witness firsthand the wonders of nature.

ACES TREEHOUSE (CHARLES CUNNIFFE ARCHITECTS), Aspen, CO, United States

Stair perspective

Aerial perspective

Rear perspective

Arctic experience

These shingle-covered pine cone units seemingly grow in the landscape, rising up on their black stick legs and peering curiously at the landscape and the northern lights. The perfect spot to experience both nature and Arctic mysticism.

Designed to appear in pairs on the steep hillside, the timber structures are covered in wood, and bring to mind a warm nest, which was a guiding element of the planning process. The decor has deliberate details that tie it into the area and its experiential concept. The soft, warm materials used in the interior design highlight the nest-like atmosphere. Green roofs compensate for the footprint that was lost to construction, and the overall construction prioritized safe ecological impacts, including prefabrication, vital in the fragile Arctic region where vegetation growth is slow.

From the hall with its intimate dark atmosphere you step into the light main area, where the landscape opens up in its full glory. The wall facing the landscape is made completely of glass and every accommodation unit has been carefully positioned in a way that allows for the most unobstructed view of the scenery possible. Light pollution outdoors has been kept to a minimum to enable a true wilderness experience and a view of the northern lights.

The use of wood (including natural wood in the suite) gives the interior surfaces a homely feel, works well acoustically, and ensures healthy indoor air within the buildings. The decor favors wooden furniture and uses animal skins, leather, and wool in the textiles and carpets.

ARCTIC TREEHOUSE HOTEL (STUDIO PUISTO ARCHITECTS LTD.), Rovaniemi, Finland

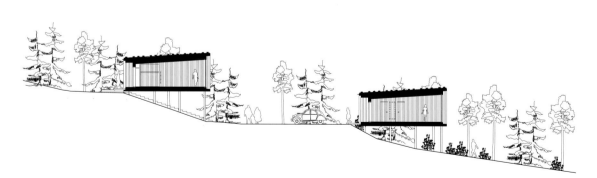

Section

Common dream

Two best friends shared a common dream to build their own tree house, creating a special hideaway for themselves and guests. They turned to Baumraum, who specializes in designing tree houses, to bring their dream into reality.

The chosen location had beautiful oak trees and a picturesque view of the valley below. The resulting design combined a traditional pitched roof with an almost black building structure within a steel frame, with large glass surfaces, resting on four pillars. All components were prefabricated in Germany before being assembled on-site in just a matter of days.

The interior employs only oiled oak for cladding and for the built-in furniture, which bestows a lovely warmth, and gives it a calm and elegant character. The open living room and bedroom make full use of the height afforded by the gable, and natural light floods in. The north side frames a picturesque view over the orchard and down to the river Thur.

Above the integrated pantry and the bathroom is a gallery with a cozy sleeping area. A skylight provides an exceptional view into the canopy of the oak and to the stars at night-time. A small wood stove creates warmth and coziness on cold days. The petite bathroom contains a beautiful stone from the nearby river, which forms a natural stone sink. All in all, this cozy and perfectly designed tree house is a dream come true for two friends.

BAUMHAUS HALDEN (BAUMRAUM), Halden, Switzerland

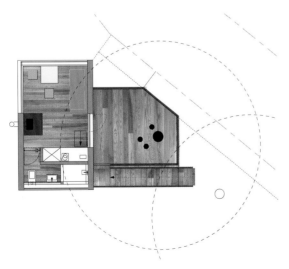

Floor plan

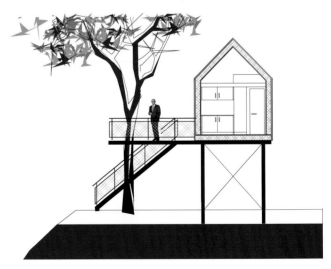

Elevation

Lofty escape

An abandoned slalom slope in northern Sweden provided the perfect spot to create the Bergaliv Landscape Hotel, comprising four beautiful cabins. The first cabin, a tall two-story loft house set high above the treetops, was constructed with panoramic views over a stunning landscape across the river valley to the mountains beyond.

Based on traditional Swedish härbre buildings used to store grains, Bergaliv Loft House is an architect-designed organic cabin that blends in with the surrounding nature and highlights its natural beauty. A top deck provides the perfect vantage point to make the most of the valley views while the accommodation level brings the visitor in close contact with the surrounding forest. The structure is lifted up off the ground by a timber framework, which continues through the building before revealing itself again in the loft component. Constructed from pale wood, the loft house stands out amid the dark foliage of the trees. The exterior is built using heart pine and spruce wood, while the interior uses birch plywood and ash. The walls are insulated with flax fibers, harnessing an old Nordic building tradition.

The interior design was strongly influenced by Japanese aesthetics to portray the idea of simplicity, allowing nature to talk and the house to be silent. It is deliberately minimalistic and raw, inviting light and space.

Whether in summer with its long days and short nights or winter when visitors can remain snug and cozy inside, before venturing out to find traces of elks, foxes, and rabbits that mark the snow, this is the perfect spot to ascend to the treetops while seeing nature from a new vantage point.

BERGALIV LOFT HOUSE (HANNA MICHELSON), Orbaden, Sweden

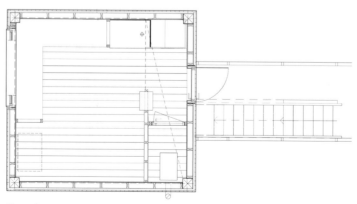

Floor plan

Tuscan delight

Taking the idea of green and sustainable architecture that one step further, Black Cabin combines a solid construction with high-tech elements, and proudly displays luxury as its watchword. This well-appointed structure, available for rent, is set within the grounds of a Tuscan olive and lavender farm, with stunning views over the rural Tuscan landscape to the Cimini Mountains and across to the sea of Tarquinia.

Nestled within the strong boughs of a 200-year-old maritime pine, the tree house was designed by French company La Cabane Perchée following an idea proposed by Renzo Stucchi. It is clad in Canadian cedar, and effortlessly oozes tranquility and a luxurious elegance. The interior is designed by Claudia Pelizzari from Archiglam, employing contrasting colors and natural fabrics, such as linen and cotton, and using materials in unusual combinations, such as wood, glass, and steel, creating a glamorous and ultraluxe look. The shower is decorated with Corian marble and crystal. Careful attention to detail pervades the design, and includes a Bose home theater system, LED lights, and heating/air conditioning.

The owners wanted to explore the idea of a tree house being more than a fable or figment of imagination, and have created what they describe as an eco-loft, suspended from the tree. The design carefully does not impose or damage any part of the tree, and in return, the structure is shaded from the hot sun. The result is a holiday retreat that allows one to enjoy the sense of nature, but with all the comforts still available. The perfect place to escape, unwind, and regenerate.

BLACK CABIN (LA CABANE PERCHÉE), Tuscany, Italy

Chapel on the river

Treehouse Utopia is a unique tree-house destination, with four arboreal hideaways available to stay in, offering a chance to reconnect with nature and feel the warm embrace of the tree canopy. Successfully combining the enthusiasm of the inner child with the grown-up's wish for luxury and comfort, each of the rentable tree houses tick all the boxes and are infused with their own theme and personality.

Chapelle, like its siblings, is constructed in old and venerable bald cypress pine trees, situated on the banks of the crystal-clear Sabinal River. The Chapelle has a spiritual feeling about it with its deep reds, metallic embroideries, and endless flameless candles. Access is via an angled wooden staircase.

Inside, it is hard to believe this is a tree house. Warm colored rugs adorn the wooden floor, chandeliers sparkle at night, Gothic touches are everywhere while sash windows let you gaze outside.

The treetop getaway lets you get up close to the native wildlife and the sunsets are a captivating sight, whether viewed from the inside or while ensconced on a comfy outdoor lounge outside on the deck.

Ascending to the heights of the cypress does not mean leaving civilization entirely behind. Each structure comes complete with not only a bedroom (with a queen-size bed), but a sitting room as well as a full bathroom (Chapelle boasts a claw-foot bath tub and a bijou stained-glass window) with shower, and a terrace to soak up the natural surroundings outside. Air conditioning and heating keep you cool or toasty warm, and there is Wi-Fi. Perfect for sharing that amazing picture on social media.

CHAPELLE (TREEHOUSE UTOPIA), Utopia, TX, United States

Treetop castles

Comprising six luxurious tree houses, this tree hotel resort is set in a beautiful wooded landscape in southern France in the Périgord region. All are available for rent, with gourmet regional delights to select from. All were designed and constructed by French company Nid Perché, experts in creating spectacular tree houses and with an impressive résumé. Each tree house contains its own unique character.

Château Hautefort is the largest tree house built so far. With its shingle roof and dormer windows, the structure rests in a centenarian oak tree. Able to accommodate six people, the interior is spacious and includes a functional (if petite) kitchen. A wooden footbridge across the moats leads into a spacious internal courtyard. The theme here is early twentieth century, with ironwork chairs on the terrace and the windows featuring iron openings of that period. The double bed is a simple cast-iron one, perfectly in keeping with the overall period theme and mirroring the traditional iron work that stamps its authority and patina on the internal atmosphere.

Château Puybeton offers a stunning opportunity to rest among the trees. The genuine originality of the architecture is different to the other tree houses in the hotel, and it is hard to remember at times that you are high in the trees. A night here amid the trees allows you to contemplate the panorama of the dense and mysterious treetops. The interior design is darker than the other styles, with black punctuating the color scheme. A spacious bathroom, with two pedestal sinks and a cast-iron clawfoot bathtub, lets you to truly sink back and relax. Or, perhaps enjoy some time in the Jacuzzi looking out across the majestic oak forest.

CHÂTEAUX DANS LES ARBRES (NID PERCHÉ), Domaine de Puybeton, France

Inspired geometry

When the client requested a cabin-like, one-bedroom hideaway resembling a tree house to be built on their tree-rich property, the architects were inspired by the surrounding trees, and also the timber cabins of Horace Gifford and that master of working with the void or in-between space, Kengo Kuma. The result is an eye-catching beautiful timber-clad cylindrical structure.

The design also drew on influences such as Louis I. Kahn and his mastery of pure form, and the detailing ethic of Carlo Scarpa, to produce a process of geometric restraint and handcrafted manufacturing.

Located in a small clearing among the forest-like garden, the resulting structure explores the geometry of a square while responding similarly to the verticality of the surrounding trees in order to maximize views. The building became a vertically arranged "clearing in the forest," with living space on the first level, a bedroom placed on the second level and a roof deck on the third. The half-round bays accommodate a patio, dining alcove and stairs on the first level, and a bathroom on the bedroom level. The building sits lightly on the ground, its height accentuating the feeling of being among the trees. Entry is by means of a suspended timber and Corten steel ramp, adding to the sense of adventure.

The interior is bathed in natural light, with generous glazed windows, while the warm timber tones form a delightful contrast to the verdant canopy outside. The connections between steel and timber are expressed by means of handturned brass components. All materials are left untreated, and will express the passing of time as they weather naturally within the surrounding environment.

CONSTANTIA TREEHOUSE (MALAN VORSTER ARCHITECTURE INTERIOR DESIGN), South Africa

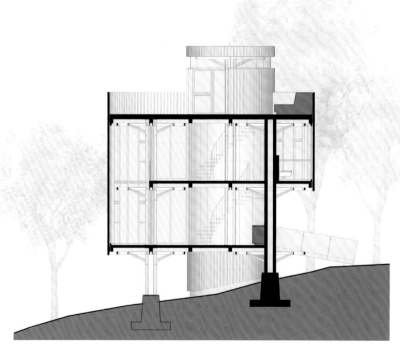

Section

Jungle living

With its design inspired by the jungle of its densely forested site, this stunning residence is built entirely of locally harvested teak wood, and includes beautiful slatted walls. Owned by surfers with a strong environmental outlook, the project reflects their deep commitment to sustainable land management. Designed with an intentionally small footprint, the residence sits lightly on the site while engaging with the natural landscape in different ways on each of its three levels.

This open-air surfer hut engages the Costa Rican landscape in various ways, from the jungle vegetation accessible just off the main floor, to the larger weather and surf patterns one can experience on the top level. The middle level nestles within the trees, giving an impression of being in a tree house, while the top levels soars above the tree canopy, providing views of the surf off nearby Playa Hermosa.

The passive home is intended to breathe and remain open to the elements in this temperate semi-tropical environment. The slatted walls allow ventilation and natural light to penetrate into the interior, while there are also whole walls that can slide open, bringing the external nature into the inside. The large roof made of wood and metal extends beyond the building, providing shade and protection during frequent tropical rainstorms.

The interior is clad in wooden panels and, befitting a holiday retreat, is sparsely furnished with easy-to-maintain simple furniture. The tree house element is evoked strongly through the use of tree trunks as columns, providing a rustic atmosphere. In a country known for its jungle rainforests and scenic coastline, this retreat provides a close-up into the best of both, particularly on the second level, which is the only space to include glass windows so the inhabitants can truly appreciate the outlook.

COSTA RICA TREEHOUSE (OLSON KUNDIG), Playa Hermosa, Costa Rica

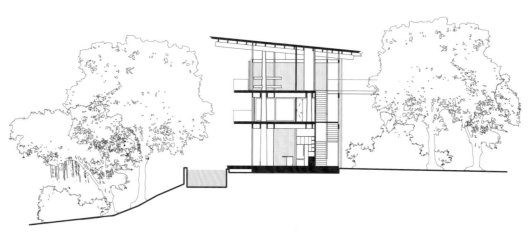

Section

Designer hideout

At first glance, you'd be forgiven for imagining the Crump Treehouse in the middle of the Australian bush. Nestled among peppermint gums and casuarinas, it was conceived as an A-framed hideout for the architect's two boys and their neighborhood friends. Located just down the hill from the family home, this is a true designer hideout, one that kids and adults alike might dream about.

Set on a steep sloping site overlooking Hobart and the Derwent River, the project was built largely from recycled building materials as an exercise in getting the most from as little as possible.

Accessed by a series of floating timber duck-boards, a towering mature gum tree supports the tree house on one side while the sheer slope of the adjacent hill supports the other. The tree house consists of an entry deck and a single, versatile room with a small loft, accessed by a ladder above.

Pitched at 70 degrees, the steep roof defines the form of the building, and allows for increased interior height and a usable loft space, within the roof's small footprint.

Complete with daybed and fireplace, the tree house projects a classic childhood image of home. It is a tiny house for the little and big people in the architect's family and provides a secret place to escape.

CRUMP TREEHOUSE (CRUMP ARCHITECTS), Hobart, Tas, Australia

Floor plan

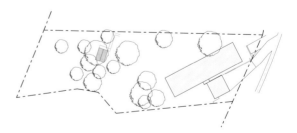

Site plan

Across the canopy

With these stunning geodesic domes, one can enjoy glamping in the treetops in the beautiful region of Quebec, overlooking the Saint Lawrence River.

The structures are designed to sit lightly on the terrain, and provide an oasis of comfort amid the tree canopy, where the inhabitant can enjoy the changing colors of the seasons, snug and secure within. Each dome is autonomous, yet all offer an eco-luxurious camping experience, close to the unique and unspoilt natural surroundings.

The domes have been carefully placed with consideration to the mountain slope, and are lifted up above the ground on a wooden platform. Modern facilities are included, as well as two large beds, as well as a spa located outside on the timber deck. The opening to the south offers a panoramic view down to the river and across the tree canopy. It also allows natural light indoors.

The interior is decorated with a minimalist black color tone, lending an air of modernism and comfort. The material covering the dome is a lovely white on the outside, but a calming gray on the inside that combined with the warmth of the wood tones creates a warm and cozy ambiance.

Either stretching out on the capacious bed on the lower level, with spectacular views, or enjoying breakfast at the table, one can imagine you are in a space-age luxurious tree house, atop of the world.

DÔMES DE CHARLEVOIX (BOURGEOIS / LECHASSEUR ARCHITECTES), Quebec, Canada

Cross section

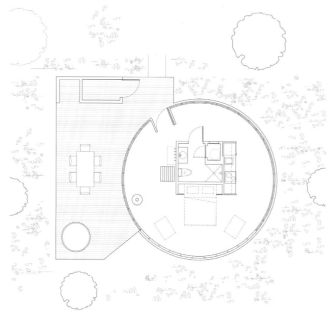

Floor plan

Woodland wonder

Located in Hot Springs and nestled in a natural hillside alongside Lake Hamilton, this stunning tree house is a welcome addition to the Evans Children's Adventure Garden, within Garvan Woodland Gardens, and is the first of three ultimately planned to grace the grounds.

Designed as part of an ambitious plan to entice children back into the woods, the tree house uses a rich visual and tactile environment to stimulate mind and body, and to strengthen connections back to the natural world. The architects were able to draw on their own childhood experiences from growing up in mostly rural settings and merge this with the firm's philosophy of "think, make, do" to produce a unique structure that accommodates the needs of all users.

The form and program of the structure was driven by the underlying theme of dendrology: the study of trees and wooded plants. The screen creates a semitransparent shell, and comprises 113 fins made from thermalized Arkansas-sourced Southern yellow pine wood. This evocative form dynamically shrouds multiple levels of spaces for both children and adults alike, and refocuses their attention to the natural wonders of the surrounding forest canopy. In this way, children who have become disconnected from playing in nature and have little knowledge of the forests, insects, and animals of Arkansas may be drawn in to observe at a close distance.

This mysterious form, with its creative play of shadow and light and enticing sense of exploration and adventure, becomes a magical experience within the Ouachita forest, and easily blends in among the native pines and oaks.

EVANS TREE HOUSE (MODUS STUDIO), Hot Springs, AR, United States

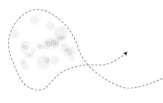

a place in the trees

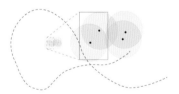

a place to play

in a site rich with colors,
forms, and textures

a place that plays, squeezing
between the trees

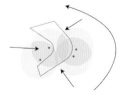

pulled by the bridge and
pushed by the trees

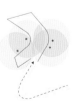

balanced between rigid garden geometry
and organic softness, while being
connected to the site

Connected to nature

Set amid a forested glade, this wooden home offers the sense of living among the tree canopy. Its nine supports stretch deep into the hillside, like roots, leaving the structure to stand tall on a vertical slope in the heights of Mexico City. The result is a home that feels like living in a tree house.

Inspired by the surrounding trees, Floating House is much more than the sum of all its spaces. It forms a bridge between nature and shelter, inviting the trees and plants inside. Designed to reflect the surrounding nature, the aim is not to dominate but rather surrender to the natural surrounds.

The construction is modest, exchanging size and quality for the benefit of lightness and integration, resulting in a beautiful building that is at home here in nature. Constructed largely of wood, the texture absorbs the local materials, and transforms them into an experience. The integration between the outside and the interior is of prime importance and as such the interior has been left deliberately raw and undecorated.

With the stairs spiraling around the house on the outside, the inhabitant can ascend through the house between the studio and the bedroom. Each new step provides access to different views and sensations.

The house glows with the warmth of the wood, and hiding within its vertical spiral is perfectly at home in the depths of its surroundings.

FLOATING HOUSE (TALLERESQUE), Mexico City, Mexico

East elevation

South elevation

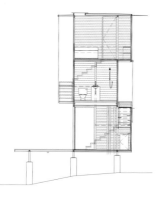

Cross section

Patchwork of glass

Harnessing the proven and tested method of constructing a tree house in the old days from whatever material was to hand, this beautiful design uses salvaged materials to create an entirely new concept. Created by interior designer Christina Salway and Nelson Treehouse & Supply, the structure is the result of sourcing old windows and weaving them together in a patchwork of new walls.

The windows have the added bonus of providing unobstructed views of the surrounding landscape. Christina appreciates the aesthetic of the salvaged vintage windows, with their old chipped wooden frames, and the windows that adorn this tree house were a mixture of found pieces and others that were donated by friends and family.

An added extra is the brass slide pole, which her young son adores, as well as a five-person hammock situated underneath the tree house. The slanted roof provides a double-height living area, and allows for the patchwork quilt of windows to be seen at their best, while letting in lots of natural light. A deck surrounding the tree house is the perfect spot to sit and sip a cup of tea, while soaking up the countryside from above.

The internal furnishings are a beautiful cacophony of color and texture, and the result of finding many objects secondhand that become statement pieces in their own right. Combing old and new pieces creates a unique space that truly reflects the family's story, and integrates items that are of personal significance.

GLASSHOUSE TREEHOUSE (ELEVENTWOELEVEN DESIGN), Catskills Mountains, NY, United States

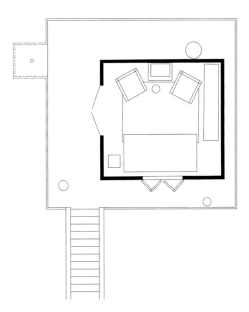

Floor plan

Lakeside living

Located just outside the town of Woodstock, less than two hours' drive from New York City, the Inhabit tree house looks out over the magnificent Catskills mountain range, quietly nestled within the dense woodland forest. The cedar-clad tree house features a large window offering superb views of the surrounding woodland and mountains.

The owner was captivated by the conceptual design prepared by Antony Gibbon, and commissioned this beautiful structure with the aim of uniting the building with the forest as much as possible. The external cladding, made from reclaimed cedar, will age with time, allowing the tree house to blend in with the natural surroundings. The large open windows allow ample natural light into the interior.

The wooden volume rests on a pair of angled metal beams, giving a lightness to its appearance almost as if the tree house is floating.

The space consists of an open-plan lounge, wood burner, and kitchen with a spacious loft bedroom, accessed by a ladder, above. The mezzanine bedroom enjoys a large glazed window that stretches up to the ceiling. In the rear of the building is a separate shower room and bathroom, accessed via a wood-lined hallway. A second bedroom at the rear could easily become an office studio space, if required. The structure has two balconies, either side of the kitchen/lounge area with a large terrace underneath that leads down to the lake and hot tub.

INHABIT (ANTONY GIBBON DESIGNS), Woodstock, NY, United States

Lavender fields

Commissioned by La Piantata Hotel, this delightful and rustic tree house fulfils a childhood dream of the owner, and represents an unusual form of hotel escape. Located within the hotel grounds against a background of lavender fields, this is the perfect expression of a stylish arboreal abode, and the perfect relaxing getaway from the hustle and bustle of everyday life.

Set within the branches of a century-old oak tree, the structure was designed and built by French company La Cabane Perchée based on an idea by Renzo Stucchi. In summer, the tree house is shaded by the foliage of the oak. As one might expect from a top hotel, La Suite Bleue is beautifully appointed and contains all the mod cons. And as a bonus, breakfast comes from the nearby hotel, and must be hoisted upstairs via a pulley system.

A gently winding wooden stair ascends to the accommodation suite. The double bedroom is spacious and boasts a four-poster bed (not something generally associated with tree houses). Rustic decoration touches amplify the cottage vibe while belying the luxury contained within. And yet this design is in harmony with its surrounds. The interior is clad in warm-colored wood, while the furnishings are a restful muted color, bringing to mind relaxing summer breezes.

The large terrace provides the best spot to indulge in some al fresco breakfast, or perhaps just to sit and daydream, or observe the surrounding nature. The statuesque tree ably houses the wooden volume securely in its boughs, providing a wonderful feeling of closeness to nature. By fulfilling the owner's childhood dream, La Suite Bleue allows the visitor to reside in the tree house of our childhood dreams.

LA SUITE BLEUE (LA CABANE PERCHÉE), Tuscany, Italy

Simple pleasures

This structure is deceptively simple, yet its purpose is large: it is a bid to reconnect the average modern person with the nature and solitude that can be provided by a forest.

As in many tree houses, to gain access to the treetops is to embark upon a small journey, whether by a ramp or stairs or climbing the tree trunk. In this case, the process of reaching the structure represents an alternative path, a journey that elevates people through a century-old forest, leaving behind all hostility, and reaching in triumph the canopy of trees.

In practice, this takes the form of a long wooden ramp, that winds its way through the tall trees, before arriving at the destination. The end result of the journey is a simple cubic-shaped tree house wrapped around a single tree trunk, with a terrace at the front. This provides space for a small fire and also to sit and dangle your legs while gazing out to the broader views, observing nature and enjoying the peaceful solitude that a forest can offer.

With this project, the beauty is not only in the surrounding majestic tall trees, but the simplicity of the basic form, a shelter reduced to its most basic form to focus on the goal of the design. From here, with no distractions, one can focus on the wonder of nature, and have the perfect perch to see the sun set through the trees.

LESOM (SOZONYCH), Kostroma, Russia

Uplifting experiment

This uplifting project is a small experimental treetop boutique hotel, located on the beautiful island of Bali. It provided a testing ground for the firm to explore ideas on how to lift structures off the ground, resulting in a less invasive footprint and reduced impact, with the added bonus of being more cost-effective and faster to build. The site will contain additional off-the-ground structures as time goes on, continuing to seek alternatives to vast uses of concrete that can negatively impact the environment.

The aim was to create a space where people could retreat to, a place to relax and enjoy a sense of detachment. The guests are able to enjoy 360-degree views of lush, tropical surroundings, and leave with impermeable memories.

The firm created "off-the-ground" experiences with two structures that merge traditional Balinese architecture with a surreal mix of the industrial, all embedded in a tropical forest. The tree houses are both raised above the ground on pillars, and topped with traditional thatch roof. Access is via a spiral staircase. The main spaces are decorated in a relaxed fashion, with natural color tones and an emphasis on natural materials.

In its tropical locale, the height showed the advantages of building off the ground, including enhanced passive cooling, shade from the sun provided by adjacent trees, and fewer mosquitos. At the end of the day, simply enjoying a new vantage point in such a beautiful location is priceless.

LIFT BALI (ALEXIS DORNIER), Ubud, Bali, Indonesia

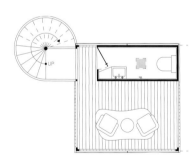

Green tower first-floor plan

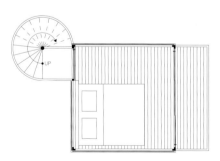

Green tower second-floor plan

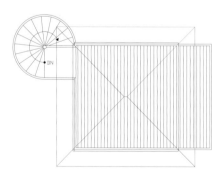

Green tower third-floor plan

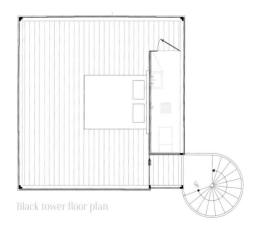

Black tower floor plan

Cozy tranquility

With Sweden's Treehotel setting the scene for hotel accommodation in the treetops, now Denmark is joining in, with its first contribution to arboreal hotel rooms.

Comprising nine cabins at present, these are built in a small, quaint forest, a mix of deciduous and coniferous trees with soft moss on the forest floor, on the Als Odde peninsula. The cabins are situated on a small hilltop, overlooking a meadow, providing a wonderful view over the tops of the trees. If you are quiet, you may spy deer, rabbits, or pheasants from your cozy cabin vantage point.

Each hotel room is a cabin high up in the trees. Each cabin can host up to four sleeping guests and encloses a tree which grows up through the middle. The access to the roof terrace gives the impression that you continue to "climb" the tree to reach the canopy. In all directions scenic views of the forest are framed by panoramic windows. The interior is light and bright, and compactly set out. There is also a deck terrace, complete with outdoor chairs and tables, so you can observe the forest at length. An outdoor shower is mounted on the façade of the cabin to create the experience of bathing in the forest among the trees.

LOVTAG (SIGURD LARSEN), Als Odde, Denmark

Floor plan

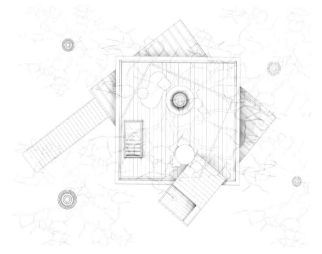

Roof plan

Reflective ambitions

The renowned Treehotel, located in the far north of Sweden, close to the polar circle, is represented here by the stunning Mirrorcube. Completed in 2010, its photogenic properties have led to it becoming famous across the world.

During the design, Tham & Videgård sought to explore the relationship between people and nature, and also how humans use high-tech materials and products to explore remote places in harsh climates. The firm approaches nature both as something enticing, but also cognizant of the challenges it can present.

The Mirrorcube can in truth be described as a simple hut in the trees, a lightweight aluminum structure mounted directly on the tree trunk of a tall pine, but it is so much more. The entire volume is clad in mirrored glass, such that the exterior reflects the surroundings and the sky, creating a camouflaged place among the treetops. The interior is all made of plywood and the windows give a 360-degree view of the surroundings. The structure can be viewed as a paradox of the search for an original and authentic experience, combined with high-tech materials that we believe we need in order to get really close to nature.

The cabin offers accommodations for two people; a king-size bed, a small kitchenette and bathroom, as well as a living room and a roof terrace. Access is via a rope ladder or a rope bridge attached to the adjacent trees.

Built using local materials and resources, the designers also carefully considered the dangers posed by the reflective glass to the birdlife. As such, to prevent birds colliding with the reflective glass, a transparent ultraviolet color is laminated into the glass panes, which is visible to birds only.

MIRRORCUBE (THAM & VIDGÅRD ARKITEKTER), Harads, Sweden

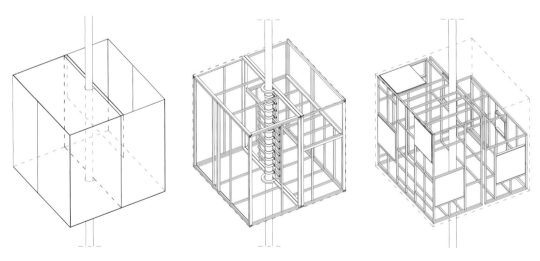

Axonometric sequence

Pinecone peek-a-boo

The spruce trees in this old forest in Italy may be renowned for the quality of their wood (sought after in making violins), but the pinecones they produce are often small compared to their pine tree cousins. Until now. This new addition to a mountain retreat dwarfs any competition, and sits supported by surrounding fir trees as if it just fell from a (very large) tree. The project stemmed from a desire to create a refuge that was also a natural element of its environment.

Suspended over 30 feet (10 meters) above the ground, and accessible via a wooden walkway, the architect describes his design as a "house without foundations." The circular shape is designed to help the inhabitants feel connected to nature at all times. Made from wood sourced directly from the area, the frame is built from cross-laminated timber, and insulated with breathable wood fiber. The larch shingle cladding, small in size to easily follow the curvature of the impressive tree-house form, also mimics pinecone scales.

Each house is arranged over three levels, with the first forming a panoramic covered terrace. The second level comprises the living areas, and includes a small balcony, while the top level contains the bedroom, which glories in the warmth of the wooden paneling, and has a skylight above the bed, allowing for comfortable night-time gazing at the starry sky.

PIGNA (ARCHITETTO BELTRAME CLAUDIO), Malborghetto, Italy

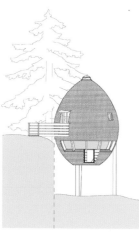

Pigna I entry elevation

Pigna I front elevation

Pigna I section

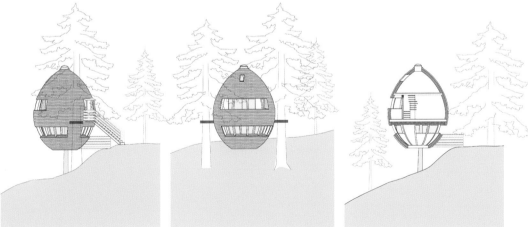

Pigna 2 entry elevation   Pigna 2 front elevation   Pigna 2 section

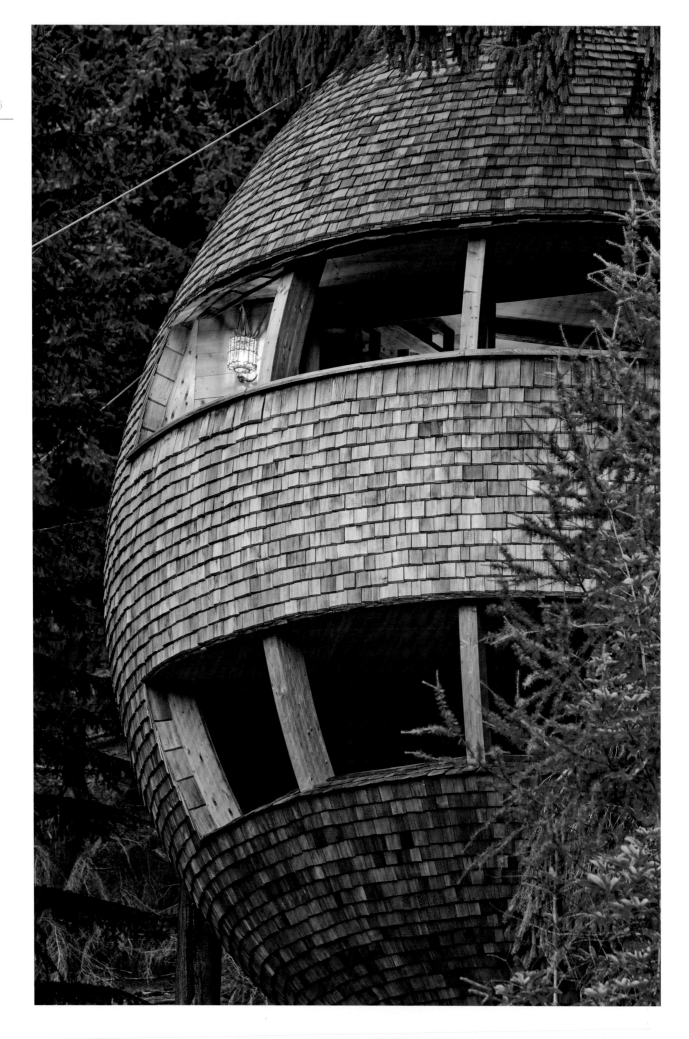

Summer garden retreat

Perched on the edge of the garden within walking distance of the pool lies the Pool View Treehouse. Crafted seamlessly from premium-grade cedar shingles and cladding, which will fade into a silvery shade to blend in with its surroundings, the tree house offers captivating views over the pool and garden.

The client wanted to add to the existing leisure area in their garden and asked us to design a unique "pool house" where the family could relax after an afternoon of swimming, but also be multifunctional so it could also be used as an impressive party venue and hangout den for their teenagers. The family loved the idea of having a luxurious and comfortable interior, fitted with all the creature comforts you could possibly wish for. Inside, the main room features a home cinema, television cabinet, and a semicircular sofa, ideal for watching films or playing the Xbox.

Finished with oak flooring and cedar lining, the interior has a light, airy and luxurious feel as well as a fragrant woody scent. There are nine handcrafted windows of various sizes to let in plenty of sunlight. In the summer, double doors can be opened, helping the inside and outside spaces to merge. The tree house includes a cozy sleeping loft on a mezzanine level that is accessed via a ladder and trapdoor, ideal for sleepovers. A glass balustrade provides a great view down into the tree-house lounge, adding a sense of height and adventure.

The resulting tree house is large enough to cater for all the needs of the family, while still blending in with the undergrowth and creating a beautiful one-of-a-kind feature for the client's property.

POOL VIEW TREEHOUSE (BLUE FOREST), Surrey, United Kingdom

Floor plan

Building on traditions

Embedded into the tropical landscape of San Jose del Cabo, a group of thirteen tree houses rise up into the palm trees. The boutique hotel provides a rural experience of tranquility and a direct connection with the nature of Los Cabos, while respecting the protected natural environment. Each tree house is elevated high above the ground level on elegant metal columns, which safely places the accommodations above potential flooding during the rainy season (including hurricanes) while also guaranteeing privacy for the users. The metal structure reduces the intervention impact on the natural landscape, important in this protected environment.

Each unit is formed by a compact box, in a complex set of layers formed by the basic steel structure, the mosquito net panels and the palo de arco rods (local wood) creating comfortable conditions in a minimal space. Other materials like polycarbonate and polished cement are used in the bathrooms, creating an aesthetic and atemporal contrast with the raw traditional materials like the palo de arco. The used materials evoke the local constructive tradition and dignify its use in the contemporaneity, in a harmonious composition between traditional and modern techniques while maintaining the same concept throughout the entire project.

Each tree house is equipped with a private bathroom, a closet, and a deck with outdoor showers where visitors can enjoy the privileged views of the Estero (west) and the Sea of Cortez (south) over the dense foliage of palm trees. The height has an added bonus. The cross ventilation allows the sea breeze to pass through the centenarian palm grove and into the units. Befitting a relaxed tropical lifestyle, residents are able to keep their doors open to capture the breeze, and also take full advantage of the spectacular views.

TREE HOUSES@ACRE (FABRIK°G), San Jose del Cabo, Mexico

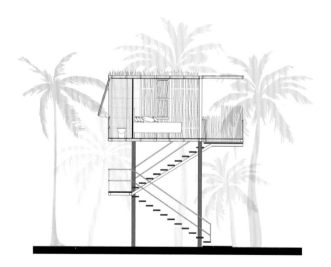

Section

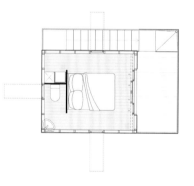

Floor plan

Thermal motivation

Tapping into the dreams of fantastic tree houses of childhood, this quite unique project emerges quietly from among the treetops. Built on piles that raise it high above the ground, the design rejects all right angles, and winds sinuously around the trunks. You can clearly see where it got its serpentine name. This unusual tourist residence is located in Pedras Salgadas Park, once known for its thermal waters. As tourist numbers dropped as thermal baths fell out of favor when the lure of the beach holiday grew, the infrastructure slowly fell into disrepair. The Tree Snake House forms part of a plan to reinvigorate the park by providing attractive accommodations that could be found nowhere else. Its markedly romantic design is typical of the peak of thermal tourism.

The external covering of slate and wood aids in camouflaging the building, and also brings to mind a snake gliding stealthily through the forest, combing the idea of a (reinterpreted) primitive hut with that of a reptile in the wild. But rather than inspire fear, this sinuous structure snaking its way through the forest offers modern and comfortable eco-friendly accommodations. Comprising a bedroom and sitting room, bathroom, and kitchen, the interior is surprisingly roomy, with a palette of cool light colors accented by the warmth of wood. New technology allows the weightless easy-carrying construction to bear the load easily of the house, while local raw material, slate and wood are used in the finish to promote its integration into the environment.

The round front window, framing a view over the surrounding trees, and the skylight, offering a segment of the sky, articulate in exemplary fashion the idea of the human condition, between heaven and earth.

TREE SNAKE HOUSE (LUIS REBELO DE ANDRADE), Vila Pouca de Aguiar, Portugal

Playing with the aspect

Located on a hill in a pine forest, and placed lightly between trees is this residence that was designed as a livable tree house. Eco-friendly to its core, the result is a modern home, with an elevation and construction details that all combine to resemble a tree house, albeit with all the mod cons and comfort provided.

The home is elevated through the use of deep screw piles to preserve the roots of the surrounding trees and lessen the overall impact on the environment. The rectangular volume is clad externally with burnt wood that resembles the trunks of the pines, while generous windows allow for plenty of light within the interior and also views to the surrounding treescape. The design playfully merges the inside and outside, combining the two with interweaving volumes and with trees crossing the wooden slab. Indeed, the trees pop up in some surprising corners, helping with the belief that you are in a tree house. A patio forms the center of the residence, with the remainder of the building organizing itself around that.

The external balcony reflects the tree house of days gone by, and the installation of two rustic swings beneath adds to the sense of this being a grown-up tree house for adventure and play. Wooden stairs to the roof level give access to a suspended rope net, perfect for soaking up some rays or observing the avian visitors.

TREEHOUSE (ATELIER VICTORIA MIGLIORE), Fréhel, France

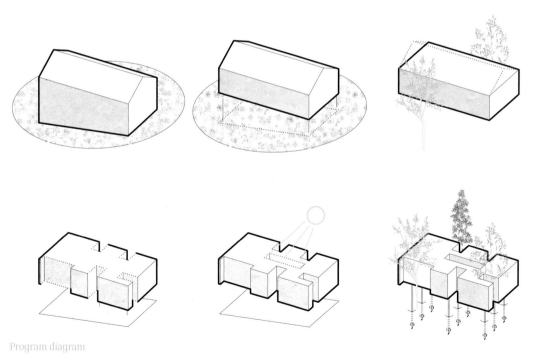

Program diagram

Pine design

When architects are provided with a challenge, you can be sure something good will result. In this case, the firm was challenged to design a tree house on a plain of pines and cork oaks. The result is this simple yet elegant elevated structure that embraces a young pine tree, and provides a vantage point overlooking the Atlantic Ocean.

The selected pine tree proved inspirational to the design: the designers assumed that the pine would serve as protection for the house and that the project would embrace the tree. Thus, it became natural to choose pine for the construction material. The raw materiality of the exterior relates to the bark of the trees and rough expression. By contrast and due to the choice in its finish, the same material resulted in a lightweight and soft interior. A system of screens guarantees a certain level of shelter and privacy to the inhabitant. The interior is sparsely furnished, allowing the natural beauty of the landscape to become the focus, and letting the sunshine highlight the color of the internal pine wood. All necessities are catered for, creating a space to enjoy the views without compromising comfort.

During the day, the broad sweep of the horizon can be best appreciated. At night, the eye is drawn naturally toward the heavens, since there are few other sources of light beyond that of the stars. In this way, the house offers different experiences throughout the day and change of source of natural light. Befitting a retreat, the spatial organization along with the tree canopy all help to filter the rising sunlight, providing the key conditions for a long and natural awakening. In addition, the balcony becomes a desirable place to enjoy the gradual sunset over the water. Simplicity was the key requirement from the client, resulting in a space to breathe, see, and feel nature.

TREE HOUSE (MADEIGUINCHO), Melides, Portugal

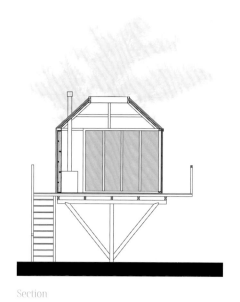

Section

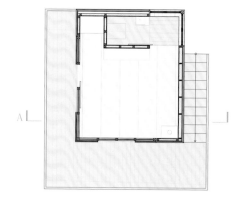

Floor plan

Backyard beauty

While tree houses are certainly versatile, and can take any form with the limit being only imagination and materials, the tree houses most commonly thought of are more humble affairs. Lovingly constructed, tree houses tend to consist of little more than some scrap wood nailed to the trunk of a tree to form steps, a platform, and perhaps some sort of railing and a roof. When a grandfather cast his mind back to his own childhood, he was inspired to create a tree house for his grandchildren, creating a space for them to enjoy and connect to nature.

His vision falls somewhere in the middle between a traditional homespun construction and one with all the bells and whistles, and brings modern sensibilities to a full-scale space. The simply named Treehouse for Grandchildren, makes use of a full-scale space on a platform. Supported by three strong trees, which grow up and through its floor and ceiling, the tree house features slatted wood walls and large openings to the outdoors to facilitate free air circulation and regulation of sunlight inside. Elevated about a full story off the ground, it's accessed by a staircase.

It feels sturdy and contemporary, ready to be glassed in for use as guest quarters or a backyard studio once the children are grown. The contrast of light and pale wood tones gives its interior a lot of visual interest, too, and a sizable deck offers further space for play.

TREEHOUSE FOR GRANDCHILDREN (MADEIGUINCHO), Cascais, Portugal

East elevation

South elevation

Counting on the view

In a situation that does not occur every day, a count contacted a tree house architect to create a set of innovative residential accommodations on his own estate. The complex consists of three large stilt houses on the edge of a small forest. The landscape around the small forest is characterized by slightly curved meadows of the golf course, hedges, smaller groups of trees, and the typical East Frisian landscape with a great view.

The three stilt houses are carefully integrated into the existing tree population. The wooden houses and terraces rest on a steel structure with straight and sloping columns. The design forms a modern interpretation of the traditional saddle-roofed house, with an almost black façade.

A branch graphic on the large glass surfaces was developed together with the nature conservationists to enable the birds to visually perceive the transparent surfaces and thus protect our feathered friends from an impact.

The interior of the stilt houses also features the design concept of anthracite-colored fixtures and natural larch on the walls and roof surfaces. On the first level there is the spacious living and dining area, a bedroom with a bunk bed for two people, a bathroom and a fully functional kitchenette with dining table. The underfloor heating based on geothermal energy and the well-insulated outer shell provide warmth and comfort even on very cold days.

A special experience for the guests is the open gallery with the sleeping area on the second level. Here they enjoy a spectacular view of the treetops and the open landscape through the large glass areas.

TREEHOUSE HOTEL LUETETSBURG (BAUMRAUM), Luetetsburg, Germany

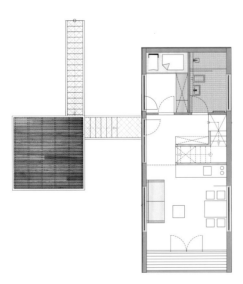

Lower floor plan

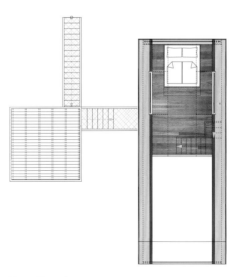

Upper floor plan

Out of this world

ZYJ Tree House World was dreamt up as a campsite style resort villa. The first phase consists of fifteen sets of independent villa-style rooms. The second phase, known as Treehouse in Qiyun Mountain, sought to provide a place that would appeal to children while providing somewhere safe for them to play.

Situated on a ridge, the new set of wooden structures take the theme of a UFO, an element from science fiction sure to attract the interest of children. The resort buildings are elevated on stilts and are spread out, connected by raised wooden walkways. The entrance to the resort is through a stone circle, above which a large silver flying saucer is suspended.

The main accommodations are luxuriously appointed, and the beautifully crafted wooden volume forms a UFO shape; the wood will fade over time and blend in with the surrounding forest. Various interior design details continue the theme of the world of flying saucers, from the constellation of stars on the bedroom ceiling to images of aliens at the foot of the bed. To cope with the rainy weather, the architects increased the depth of the eaves and added a circle of porch, forming a sheltered space for inhabitants to rest and soak up the views. The surrounding pine forest provides a sense of tranquility and isolation as the residents relax in a sea of green, far from the hue and cry of modern life.

Three other additions radiate off the main pavilion, each continuing the sci-fi theme and meant to represent passing planets. The first circle is known as the UFO Burner, which then leads to the Starry Sky Bar, covered with a white waterproof roofing. The last satellite is a trampoline, just right for children who want to test the theory of gravity.

TREEHOUSE IN QIYUN MOUNTAIN (ATELIER DESIGN CONTINUUM), Xiuning, China

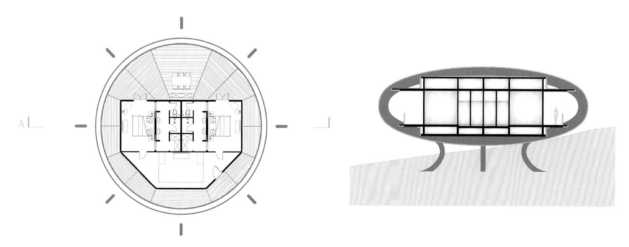

Floor plan   Cross section

Over the water

The site for this tree house, which provides joy for the family and their friends, is set within the grounds of a restored old forester's house. The surroundings were carefully landscaped to include indigenous trees and two large artificial ponds, which have provided a haven for flora and fauna alike.

The family turned to Baumraum, who is something of a specialist when it comes to designing innovative tree houses. A stand of hemlock spruce by the side of the lower pond was selected as the site. To make it more impressive, the decision was taken to create a two-story tree house tower that rested in the pond itself, and was connected to the stand of trees by means of a long terrace.

Two of the trees pierce the terrace to welcome visitors to the tree house. From this vantage point, the narrow deck of larch wood seems to float above the water of the pond until it reaches the rounded tree-house tower. Here the visitor can choose to enter the room on the lower level or to take another exterior stairway to reach the upper sleeping area. Both levels are equipped with plenty of loungers and benches as well as storage space and electrical connections.

During the day, the tree house serves as a vantage point for observing the creatures in the water and the adjoining meadows. Fish, frogs, and even deer can be sighted from here. At night, the upper room is a comfortable place to sleep and dream and, when the skies are clear, to gaze at the stars through the domed skylight. The completed tree house not only provides joy for the residents but also a beautiful adornment to the rural site, resting serenely atop the tranquil waters of the pond.

TREEHOUSE SOLLING (BAUMRAUM), Uslar, Germany

Urban double act

This project was conceived by a grandfather and his grandson as an experiment for new housing within an urban environment that would be more in tune with nature. Tree houses are normally associated with a rural setting or natural surroundings, so the project set itself up to be different from the outset. And what is better than having one tree house? The answer surely must be to have two!

Located in the bourgeois urban environment of Berlin (itself no stranger to small and extraordinary buildings that push the envelope), the project serves as an oasis, and inspires friends and family. This particular site boasted an outstanding location bordering on a forest and positioned near two lakes.

The structures were planned to take up only the amount of space needed, and preserving the existing trees was a paramount concern. Each tree house is a cubic unit, hovering on a high base. Access is via a flight of stairs, while the building's utilities are housed at ground level in a base lined with larch slats.

The interior contains everything one could possibly need: a bathroom with a shower, a light-flooded interior featuring a kitchenette and comfortable bed, as well as some beautiful home accessories. The wood spruce panels used for the walls and ceilings have been left in their natural state.

The result is the successful creation of a place that enraptures, and is a fitting tribute to the grandfather who first proposed the scheme. The two tree houses are situated at the transition from city to countryside and thus connect both worlds—vibrant Berlin with restorative scenery.

URBAN TREEHOUSE (BAUMRAUM), Berlin, Germany

Front rendering

Back rendering

Magic in the woods

Placed carefully high up in the branches of a veteran oak, this luxurious two-story tree house offers uninterrupted vistas through the tree canopy across the Dorset woodland. This is the tree house everyone dreamt of as children, complete with magical mystery.

The Woodsman's Treehouse is built on long stilts high up among the branches of three oak trees and is a substantial structure that has been carefully designed to not stress the trees in any way, thus maintaining the delicate ecosystem.

The tree house, a fine example of wood craftsmanship, is a stylish combination of sustainable craftsmanship and luxurious interiors with a playful touch. Highlights include a sauna and hot tub on the upper deck, a revolving woodburner, an open-air tree-shower (with piping-hot water), and a stainless-steel slide. On the rear deck is positioned a wood-fired pizza oven and barbeque. A pier-like boardwalk leads into the interior, via a scorched oak door with a marine porthole and submarine locking mechanism, where a king-sized bed, a double-ended copper bath, and the rotating fireplace await. A notable feature is a window in the floor, looking down to the stream below. The thick insulating walls feature picture windows that offer woodland views, and there is a ceiling window above the bed that looks up at the impressive oak canopy above.

This tree house offers a unique opportunity to relax among the branches, enjoying and admiring them while not damaging them in any way, and looking through the woods toward the sunset.

WOODSMAN'S TREEHOUSE (GUY MALLINSON AND KEITH BROWNLIE), Dorset, United Kingdom

Diner's delight

Proving that there is no limit to what a tree house can be used for, this stunning example features high-level arboreal dining. The result of a challenge to produce an "off-the-wall" functioning restaurant to feature in a television advert, it is safe to conclude that the result is truly unique, and "off-the-tree." Situated on a site north of Auckland, the chosen tree to house this spectacular design was a large redwood. The project has been described as the tree house everyone dreamed of as children, but could only build as adults.

Taking on the theme of a tree house being reminiscent of childhood, playtime, and thence stories of imagination, the designers sought to create a space that appears theatrical with a touch of enchantment. The finished structure could be interpreted as a cocoon, or a seashell or even a lantern, a beacon glowing at night. Lighting forms an important architectural component enhancing and changing the mood, with discreet lighting within the walkway and up-lighting within the tree house, all making it seem more magical at night.

Broadly speaking, it is a simple oval form, wrapped organically around the tree trunk. But its scale and form create a memorable statement, without dominating the natural setting. The vertical fins mimic the verticality of the redwood trees, enabling the structure to blend into its setting, almost as if it were a natural growth.

Access to the tree house is via an accessible walkway set high up in the treetops while facilities are all located at ground level. The tree house is weather resistant, using acrylic sheeting fixed to the roof under the fins, and with vertical roll-down café-style blinds placed on the interior.

YELLOW TREEHOUSE RESTAURANT (PETER EISING), Auckland, New Zealand

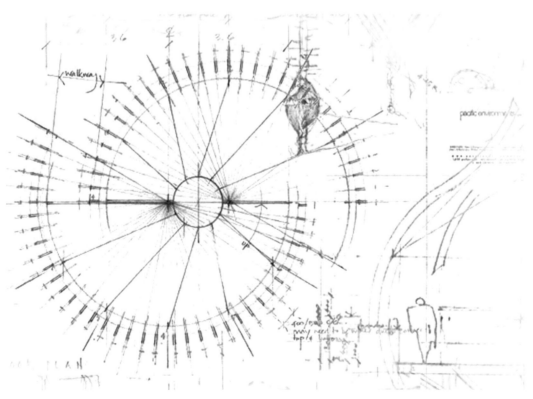

Development sketch

Rain and shine

Deep in the heart of Texas, with its rolling hills and babbling brooks, Cypress Valley hosts an eco-luxurious tree-house resort. The newest addition is Yoki Treehouse, designed by ArtisTree. Yoki is a Hopi Native American word for rain, and the structure is dedicated to the rain that renews the land. Rising high above the ground, the tree house is nestled between two old-growth bald cypress trees with a spring-fed creek burbling below.

Entry is via a second-story observation deck, where a spiral staircase leads down to the front porch, perfect for bird-watching or simply observing the beautiful surrounds. Large windows flood the open design with natural light, and illuminate the birch wood that clads the central interior. The front wall of windows creates an open immersive feeling with nature and enables guests to mingle effortlessly between the interior and exterior spaces. The intentionally simple interiors are part Japanese minimalist with select accents of Turkish decor, creating a luxurious and cozy space.

Continuing the theme of water, the bathhouse sits at the edge of the ravine and includes an onsen-style soaking tub. Each space in the retreat is curated with nature enthusiasts in mind, making it a perfect getaway from the city: a place where quiet stillness gives way to the soft cicada summer song; where there is space and time for complete introspection, innovation, and rejuvenation of the spirit. Which rather sums up the appeal of tree houses, to have a space close to nature where the stillness can be best appreciated.

YOKI TREEHOUSE (ARTISTREE), Austin, TX, United States

PROJECT CREDITS

12–19 **SUSPENDED DISBELIEF**
The 7th Room
Snøhetta || snohetta.com
LOCATION Harads, Sweden
PHOTOGRAPHY Johan Jansson

20–25 **EMBEDDED IN NATURE**
ACES Treehouse
Charles Cunniffe Architects (CCA) || cunniffe.com
LOCATION Aspen, CO, United States
PHOTOGRAPHY Ross Kribbs

26–33 **ARCTIC EXPERIENCE**
Arctic Treehouse Hotel
Studio Puisto Architects Ltd. || studiopuisto.fi
LOCATION Rovaniemi, Finland
PHOTOGRAPHY Marc Goodwin, Archmospheres /
Riikka Kantinkoski

34–41 **COMMON DREAM**
Baumhaus Halden
Baumraum || baumraum.de
LOCATION Halden, Switzerland
PHOTOGRAPHY Laura Fiorio

42–49 **LOFTY ESCAPE**
Bergaliv Loft House
Hanna Michelson || bergaliv.se
LOCATION Orbaden, Sweden
PHOTOGRAPHY Hanna Michelson

50–55 **TUSCAN DELIGHT**
Black Cabin
La Cabane Perchée || la-cabane-perchee.com ||| lapiantata.it
LOCATION Tuscany, Italy
PHOTOGRAPHY Maurizio Brera, Cinzia Stucchi

56–59 **CHAPEL ON THE RIVER**
Chapelle
Treehouse Utopia || treehouseutopia.com
LOCATION Utopia, TX, United States
PHOTOGRAPHY Treehouse Utopia

60–67 **TREETOP CASTLES**
Châteaux dans les Arbres
Nid Perché || nidperche.com
LOCATION Domaine de Puybeton, France
PHOTOGRAPHY Châteaux dans les Arbres

68–75 **INSPIRED GEOMETRY**
Constantia Treehouse
Malan Vorster Architecture Interior Design || malanvorster.co.za
LOCATION South Africa
PHOTOGRAPHY Adam Letch

76–81 **JUNGLE LIVING**
Costa Rica Treehouse
Olson Kundig || olsonkundig.com
LOCATION Playa Hermosa, Costa Rica
PHOTOGRAPHY Nic Lehoux

82–87 **DESIGNER HIDEOUT**
Crump Treehouse
Crump Architects || crumparchitects.com.au
LOCATION Hobart, Tas, Australia
PHOTOGRAPHY Andrew Knott

88–93 **ACROSS THE CANOPY**
Dômes de Charlevoix
Bourgeois / Lechasseur architectes || bourgeoislechasseur.com
LOCATION Quebec, Canada
PHOTOGRAPHY Maxime Valsan

94–101 **WOODLAND WONDER**
Evans Tree House
Modus Studio || modusstudio.com
LOCATION Hot Springs, AR, United States
PHOTOGRAPHY Timothy Hursley

102–7 **CONNECTED TO NATURE**
Floating House
Talleresque || modusstudio.com
LOCATION Mexico City, Mexico
PHOTOGRAPHY Studio Chirika

108–13 **PATCHWORK OF GLASS**
Glasshouse Treehouse
ElevenTwoEleven Design || 11211design.com
LOCATION Catskills Mountains, NY, United States
PHOTOGRAPHY ElevenTwoEleven Design

114–19 **LAKESIDE LIVING**
Inhabit
Antony Gibbon Designs || antonygibbondesigns.com
LOCATION Woodstock, NY, United States
PHOTOGRAPHY Martin Dimitrov

120–25 **LAVENDER FIELDS**
La Suite Bleue
La Cabane Perchée || la-cabane-perchee.com ||| lapianta.it
LOCATION Tuscany, Italy
PHOTOGRAPHY Maurizio Brera, Cinzia Stucchi

126–29 **SIMPLE PLEASURES**
Lesom
Sozonych || sozonych.com
LOCATION Kostroma, Russia
PHOTOGRAPHY Karmanov Evgeny

130–37   UPLIFTING EXPERIMENT
Lift Bali
Alexis Dornier || alexisdornier.com
LOCATION Ubud, Bali, Indonesia
PHOTOGRAPHY KEI

138–43   COZY TRANQUILITY
LOVTAG
Sigurd Larsen || sigurdlarsen.com
LOCATION Als Odde, Denmark
PHOTOGRAPHY Soeren Larsen

144–51   REFLECTIVE AMBITIONS
Mirrorcube
Tham & Vidgård Arkitekter || thamvidgard.se
LOCATION Harads, Sweden
PHOTOGRAPHY Åke E:son Lindman /
Lindman Photography

152–59   PINECONE PEEK-A-BOO
Pigna
Architetto Beltrame Claudio || architettobeltrame.com
LOCATION Marlborghetto, Italy
PHOTOGRAPHY Laura Tessaro, Massimo Crivellari,
Ulderica Da Pozzo

160–65   SUMMER GARDEN RETREAT
Pool View Treehouse
Blueforest || blueforest.com
LOCATION Surrey, United Kingdom
PHOTOGRAPHY Prospect Art Photography

166–73   BUILDING ON TRADITIONS
Tree Houses@ACRE
FabriK°G || fabrikg.com
LOCATION San Jose del Cabo, Mexico
PHOTOGRAPHY Gina & Ryan Photography

174–79   THERMAL MOTIVATION
Tree Snake House
Luis Rebelo de Andrade || rebelodeandrade.com
LOCATION Vila Pouca de Aguiar, Portugal
PHOTOGRAPHY FG+SG - Fotografia de Arquitectura

180–87   PLAYING WITH THE ASPECT
Treehouse
Atelier Victoria Migliore || a-vm.fr
LOCATION Fréhel, France
PHOTOGRAPHY Cyril Folliot

188–93   PINE DESIGN
Tree House
Madeiguincho || madeiguincho.pt
LOCATION Melides, Portugal
PHOTOGRAPHY João Carranca

194–99   BACKYARD BEAUTY
Treehouse for Grandchildren
Madeiguincho || madeiguincho.pt
LOCATION Cascais, Portugal
PHOTOGRAPHY João Carranca

200–7   COUNTING ON THE VIEW
Treehouse Hotel Luetetsburg
Baumraum || baumraum.de
LOCATION Luetetsburg, Germany
PHOTOGRAPHY André Dogbey

208–15   OUT OF THIS WORLD
Treehouse in Qiyun Mountain
Atelier Design Continuum || atelierdsc.com
LOCATION Xiuning, China
PHOTOGRAPHY Shao Feng

216–21   OVER THE WATER
Treehouse Solling
Baumraum || baumraum.de
LOCATION Uslar, Germany
PHOTOGRAPHY Markus Bollen

222–27   URBAN DOUBLE ACT
Urban Treehouse
Baumraum || baumraum.de
LOCATION Berlin, Germany
PHOTOGRAPHY Laura Fiorio

228–37   MAGIC IN THE WOODS
Woodsman's Treehouse
Guy Mallinson and Keith Brownlie || mallinson.co.uk ||| beandm.co
LOCATION Dorset, United Kingdom
PHOTOGRAPHY Alex Steele-Perkins

238–45   DINER'S DELIGHT
Yellow Treehouse Restaurant
Peter Eising || penzl.co.nz
LOCATION Auckland, New Zealand
PHOTOGRAPHY Lucy Gauntlett

246–51   RAIN AND SHINE
Yoki Treehouse
ArtisTree || artistreehomes.com
LOCATION Austin, TX, United States
PHOTOGRAPHY Smile Forest Photography

First reprinted 2022
The Images Publishing Group Reference Number: 1667

First published in Australia in 2021 by
The Images Publishing Group Pty Ltd
ABN 89 059 734 431

OFFICES

Australia
6 Bastow Place
Mulgrave, Victoria 3170
Australia
Tel: +61 3 9561 5544

United States
6 West 18th Street 4B
New York, NY 10011
United States
Tel: +1 212 645 1111

Shanghai
6F, Building C, 838 Guangji Road
Hongkou District, Shanghai 200434
China
Tel: +86 021 31260822

books@imagespublishing.com
www.imagespublishing.com

A catalogue record for this
book is available from the
National Library of Australia

Title: Tree Houses: Escape to the canopy
Author: Peter Eising [Introduction]
ISBN: 9781864708837

Printed and bound in China by Artron Art Group on 157gsm Chinese OJI matte art paper
Prepress (pages) by A&S Press, Singapore
Prepress image enhancement (cover) by Margit Dittes Media